The
Happiness Trap
Pocketbook

Dr Russ Harris is a medical practitioner, psychotherapist and executive coach. He grew up in the UK, but moved to Australia in his early twenties and now lives in Melbourne. He is the author of seven books, the best known being *The Happiness Trap* and *The Reality Slap*. A world-renowned trainer in Acceptance and Commitment Therapy, he has so far trained 14,000 Australian health professionals in the approach.

Bev Aisbett is an accomplished author, illustrator and exhibiting artist. Her illustrated self-help books have gained prominence with both readers and health professionals as invaluable guides to overcoming anxiety and depression, eating disorders, self-esteem issues and releasing past trauma. Since 1998, Bev has facilitated her anxiety recovery program and her work has reached thousands of sufferers through her lectures, interviews and training sessions.

The
Happiness Trap
Pocketbook

An illustrated guide on how to stop struggling and start living

Dr Russ Harris
& Bev Aisbett

EXISLE
PUBLISHING

First published 2013

Exisle Publishing Pty Ltd
PO Box 233, Gosford, NSW 2250, Australia
226 High Street, Dunedin 9016, New Zealand
www.exislepublishing.com

National Library of Australia Cataloguing-in-Publication Data:
Harris, Russ, 1966– author.
The happiness trap pocketbook : an illustrated guide on how to
stop struggling and start living / Dr Russ Harris & Bev Aisbett.
ISBN 978 1 921966 18 7 (pbk)
Happiness.
Adaptability (Psychology).
Adaptation (Physiology).
Aisbett, Bev, author
158.1

Cover design by Christabella Designs
Internal design and typesetting by IslandBridge
Typeset in Bangla MN Regular 10/14pt
Printed by Pegasus Media

This book uses paper sourced under ISO 14001 guidelines from
well-managed forests and other controlled sources.

13 15 17 19 20 18 16 14

Contents

How to use this book

Welcome to *The Happiness Trap Pocketbook*, an illustrated and simplified version of the international bestseller, *The Happiness Trap*. There are at least three ways you could use this book:

1. As an easy-to-read introduction to Acceptance & Commitment Therapy

This book presents a delightfully easy introduction to the main ideas of Acceptance & Commitment Therapy (better known as ACT). We see it as especially useful for people who are not really into reading traditional self-help books, or for those who are so stressed, anxious or depressed that reading is difficult. Of course, we hope that you will then go on to read the original book, which explores ACT in far greater depth.

2. As an adjunct to coaching or therapy

If you are seeing a coach or therapist who uses the ACT approach, this book can be a valuable adjunct. You can read chapters ahead of time to prepare for a session, or after a session as a reminder.

3. As a quick refresher course

If it's been a while since you read *The Happiness Trap*, you can use the pocketbook as a quick refresher course to remind yourself of the main ideas and exercises.

An Important Message

Simply reading this book will not be enough to make any real difference in your life. You actually will need to do the exercises if you want your life to be richer, fuller and more meaningful. It is much the same as reading a book on how to play tennis or guitar. Your tennis or guitar skills won't improve simply from reading it; you actually have to do the recommended exercises.

Of course, you can read through the book quickly and then go back and do the exercises, but it's far better to do them as you go.

So, good luck with it all. And remember: life gives most to those who make the most of what life gives.

Cheers
Russ Harris

Introduction

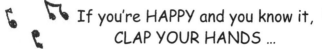

If you're HAPPY and you know it,
CLAP YOUR HANDS ...

OH DEAR!

We should be HAPPY, shouldn't we?

That's what the multitude of self-help books out there suggest — just think happy thoughts and you'll be FINE. But trying to be perpetually positive can be downright STRESSFUL!

MY DOG DIED, I LOST MY JOB, MY WIFE LEFT ME ... BUT IT'S ALL *GOOD*!

BUT ISN'T IT *NORMAL* TO BE HAPPY?

You'd think that it would be normal to be happy in the western world, where we have access to so many of the ingredients to build happiness ...

GOOD HOUSING	MORE & BETTER FOOD	EXCELLENT MEDICAL FACILITIES

ACCESS TO

EDUCATION	JUSTICE	WELFARE

CLEAN WATER	&	SANITATION

Along with FREEDOM TO

TRAVEL	SPEAK OPENLY	VOTE

But the truth is, on the whole we're NOT happy.
In fact, often we're downright MISERABLE!

Here are some sobering statistics:

1 in 10 has
CLINICAL DEPRESSION

1 in 5 is DEPRESSED
at some time

1 in 4 has or has had an
ADDICTION

30 per cent of the adult
population has a recognised
PSYCHOLOGICAL DISORDER

And of all the people you know, almost HALF of these will
SERIOUSLY CONTEMPLATE SUICIDE at some point ...

... and 1 in 10 will actually
ATTEMPT IT!

SO WHY IS IT SO *DIFFICULT* TO BE HAPPY?

TO ANSWER THAT, WE NEED TO GO BACK IN TIME TO SEE HOW OUR MINDS *EVOLVED*!

HANG ON!

WOW!!

HERE'S AN EARLY HUNTER/GATHERER. WHAT DO YOU THINK ARE HIS *NEEDS*?

HMM ... WELL, THE *BASICS* FOR SURVIVAL!

FOOD WATER SHELTER SEX

AND HE HAS AN EVEN *GREATER* PRIORITY!

DON'T GET **KILLED!**

WHAT DO YOU THINK WAS THE GREATEST *THREAT* TO SURVIVAL FOR OUR FRIEND HERE?

LET'S SEE ... WELL, BEING *ALONE* WOULD BE DANGEROUS, I GUESS!

YES! WITHOUT THE PROTECTION OF THE TRIBE, HE WOULD BE *EASY PREY*!

SO HOW DOES THIS PLAY OUT IN *MODERN TIMES*?

WE STILL FEAR *REJECTION* AND TRY TO 'PROTECT' OURSELVES BY COMPARING OURSELVES TO OTHERS!

AM I DOING ANYTHING *WRONG*?

AM I *FITTING IN*?

AM I AS *GOOD* AS OTHERS?

AND BACK THEN, THERE WAS ONLY A SMALL GROUP TO COMPARE TO!

NOW IT'S *GLOBAL*!

FOR AN AMBITIOUS ANCESTOR THE FORMULA FOR SUCCESS WAS *MORE = BETTER*

WELL THAT SURE HASN'T *CHANGED*!

AND IT SEEMS THAT NO MATTER HOW MUCH WE GET, WE STILL WANT MORE!

YES! OUR MODERN MINDS TEND TO FOCUS ON *LACK* & CREATE DISSATISFACTION!

SO WHAT *IS* THIS HAPPINESS THAT WE KEEP CHASING AFTER?

'The very purpose of life is to seek Happiness.'

Dalai Lama

'HAPPINESS' HAS TWO VERY DIFFERENT MEANINGS ...

1.
A GOOD FEELING

Because happiness feels GOOD, we CHASE it, but we find that it doesn't LAST.

And, as we shall see, a life spent chasing after this feeling is not only UNSATISFACTORY but also the harder we try to experience only pleasurable feelings, the more we feel ANXIOUS or DEPRESSED when they elude us.

2.
AN ACTIVE PHILOSOPHY

THIS SECOND DEFINITION INSTEAD FOCUSES ON CREATING A *RICH, FULL & MEANINGFUL* LIFE!

This involves ...

TAKING ACTION ON THE THINGS THAT MATTER TO US

MOVING IN THE DIRECTION OF WHAT WE SEE AS VALUABLE OR WORTHY

ENGAGING FULLY IN WHAT WE DO

IN DOING SO, WE EMBRACE LIFE IN *ALL* ITS COLOURS!

But a full human life comes with the FULL RANGE of human emotions.

OF COURSE WE ALL LIKE TO
FEEL *GOOD*, BUT DESPERATELY
TRYING TO AVOID PAINFUL
FEELINGS DOOMS US TO
FAILURE.

The fact is — life involves PAIN:

LOSS   SEPARATION   REJECTION   ILLNESS OR
OR DIVORCE   INFIRMITY

THE GOOD NEWS IS ...

You can learn to handle painful feelings by:

▶ MAKING ROOM FOR THEM

▶ RISING ABOVE THEM

▶ CREATING A LIFE WORTH LIVING.

AND WE'LL SHOW YOU HOW,
USING THE PRINCIPLES
OF *ACT: ACCEPTANCE AND
COMMITMENT THERAPY.*

Chapter 1

Fairytales

... AND THEY LIVED *HAPPILY EVER AFTER* ...

WE'LL ALL LIVE HAPPILY EVER AFTER, WON'T WE MUMMY?

HMMM ...

HAPPY ENDINGS ... we believe that's how life should be, don't we? Is this REALISTIC? Does this fit with your own experience of life?

An expectation that life should turn out 'happily ever after' is one of the ways that we find ourselves caught in the **HAPPINESS TRAP**.

LET'S EXPLORE THE FOUR MYTHS WHICH MAKE UP THE *HAPPINESS TRAP* ...

MYTH 1:
HAPPINESS IS THE NATURAL STATE FOR HUMAN BEINGS

Our culture insists that humans are naturally happy. Yet, the scary statistics regarding mental illness in the introduction to this book tell another story.

And aside from diagnosed psychiatric disorders, there are things like:

LONELINESS

SEXUAL PROBLEMS

ILLNESS

WORK STRESS

BULLYING

PREJUDICE

LOW SELF-ESTEEM

CHRONIC ANGER

LACK OF MEANING

MID-LIFE CRISIS

SOCIAL ISOLATION

SO LASTING HAPPINESS IS ACTUALLY QUITE *RARE*, YET MANY OF US HAVE A BELIEF THAT ...

EVERYONE IS HAPPY EXCEPT *ME*!

... A BELIEF THAT CREATES EVEN *GREATER* UNHAPPINESS!

MYTH 2:
IF YOU'RE NOT HAPPY, YOU'RE DEFECTIVE

I MUST BE REALLY *MESSED UP*!

Our society tends to assume that psychological suffering is ABNORMAL: a sign of a WEAKNESS or ILLNESS and a mind that is FAULTY or DEFECTIVE.

YOU SHOULDN'T BE FEELING SO ANXIOUS.

OH NO! I MUST BE *MENTALLY ILL*!

This means that, when we inevitably experience painful thoughts and feelings, we BEAT UP on ourselves for doing so.

I'M *WEAK*!

I'M *STUPID*!

BUT AS YOU WILL SEE, YOUR MIND IS JUST DOING THE JOB IT HAS *EVOLVED* TO DO!

ACT PRINCIPLE:

THE *NORMAL* THINKING PROCESSES OF A *HEALTHY* MIND NATURALLY CREATE PSYCHOLOGICAL SUFFERING!

MYTH 3:
TO CREATE A BETTER LIFE, WE MUST GET RID OF NEGATIVE FEELINGS

The current trend of a 'feel-good' society tells us to ELIMINATE 'negative' feelings and ACCUMULATE the 'positive'.

 But in reality, the things we value most in life give rise to a whole RANGE of feelings — PLEASANT and UNPLEASANT.

For instance, in a long-term relationship, there may be JOY ...

... but also FRUSTRATION.

Anything that's MEANINGFUL in our lives will bring with it ... both pleasure *and* pain!

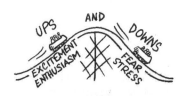

Living life to the full means experiencing UNCOMFORTABLE FEELINGS along the way. Learning how to HANDLE these feelings is essential.

MYTH 4:
YOU SHOULD BE ABLE TO CONTROL
WHAT YOU THINK AND FEEL

Many current self-help programs subscribe to this myth by:

REPLACING 'NEGATIVE' THOUGHTS
WITH 'POSITIVE' ONES

DOING AFFIRMATIONS ...   ... OR VISUALISATIONS

EVERYTHING IS
HUNKY-DORY!

The basic theme behind these approaches is:

'THINK HAPPY THOUGHTS AND YOU'LL BE HAPPY'.

If only life was that SIMPLE! Over one hundred thousand
years of evolution tend to override a few affirmations!

Even though you
might be able to
master positive
thinking when you
are relatively CALM,
negative thoughts
will start to creep in
again when you feel
STRESSED.

*ANGER
SADNESS
INSECURITY
GUILT*

*LA LA LA
HAPPY
HAPPY*

They go away, then they're back.
They go away, then they're back
— and the battle to keep them at
bay can be STRESSFUL in itself!

*AARGH!
CAN'T BE
SAD/
ANGRY/
UPSET!*

These four basic myths set us up for a battle we can NEVER WIN.

SO ARE YOU SAYING THAT NEGATIVE THOUGHTS AND FEELINGS ARE *NORMAL*?

YES. LIFE INVOLVES *PAIN*.

THEN HOW DID THESE MYTHS BECOME SO *ENTRENCHED* IN OUR CULTURE?

BECAUSE WE HAVE SO MUCH *CONTROL* OVER THE MATERIAL WORLD WE EXPECT TO HAVE *CONTROL* OVER OUR INTERNAL WORLD, BUT THIS IS *UNREALISTIC*.

TRY THESE EXPERIMENTS AND YOU'LL *SEE*!

1. DON'T THINK ABOUT ICE-CREAM FOR 30 SECONDS. DON'T THINK ABOUT ITS COLOUR, TEXTURE OR TASTE.

DON'T THINK ABOUT IT! *DAMN*!

2. LOOK AT THIS STAR FOR ONE MINUTE, BUT AS YOU DO, DON'T THINK ABOUT IT!

DAMN!

3. IMAGINE SOMEONE POINTS A GUN AT YOUR HEAD, AND SAYS 'YOU MUST FEEL NO ANXIETY — OR I WILL SHOOT YOU!'

I GUESS IT WOULD BE *CURTAINS* FOR ME!

4. CONJURE UP A MEMORY. NOW FORGET IT.

CAN'T.

5. FEEL THE INSIDE OF YOUR MOUTH. NOW MAKE IT NUMB.

I CAN STILL FEEL IT.

From an early age, we are taught that we should be able to CONTROL OUR FEELINGS:

DON'T CRY	STOP FROWNING	STOP FEELING SORRY FOR YOURSELF	THERE'S NO NEED TO BE SCARED

And this is REINFORCED as we get older.

YOU BIG SISSY!	CHILL OUT!	SNAP OUT OF IT!	DON'T BE SUCH A CHICKEN!

The implication is that you should be able to flick a switch and turn your feelings on or off at WILL.

BUT WHY IS THIS *MYTH* SO COMPELLING?

BECAUSE OTHERS *SEEM* TO BE IN CONTROL OF THEIR FEELINGS.

The reality is that most people hide their inner struggles behind a MASK OF COPING ...

WORRY WORRY WORRY

NO *WORRIES MATE*!

... and this false front adds to the ILLUSION of CONTROL.

Chapter 2

Vicious cycles

What's happening in your life?

I HAVE RELATIONSHIP PROBLEMS!

I HATE MY JOB!

I'M LONELY.

I HAVE HEALTH ISSUES.

I FEEL REJECTED.

I'VE LOST CONFIDENCE!

I'M AN ADDICT!

I'M IN FINANCIAL CRISIS!

I'M JUST STUCK!

I'M ANXIOUS!

I'M DEPRESSED!

WELL I HAVE EVERYTHING I NEED BUT I'M UNHAPPY.

Whatever the problem is, it gives rise to UNPLEASANT THOUGHTS and FEELINGS which you try to GET RID OF.

I'VE TRIED TO *IGNORE* THEM!

I'VE TRIED TO *ELIMINATE* THEM!

I'VE TRIED TO *BLOT* THEM *OUT*!

THESE ATTEMPTS TO GET RID OF UNWANTED FEELINGS ARE MAKING THEM *WORSE*!

WHAT DO YOU MEAN?

The more you try to GET RID OF, AVOID or ESCAPE feelings, the BIGGER they become.

I'M AFRAID OF REJECTION.

AND IF I SOCIALISE I MIGHT BE REJECTED!

SO I AVOID SOCIAL SITUATIONS.

SO I FEEL EVEN *MORE* REJECTED!

We have two main ways of trying to avoid painful thoughts and feelings: FIGHT or FLIGHT.

FIGHT

Trying to fight against unwanted thoughts/feelings by:

SUPPRESSION

You forcefully push away unwanted thoughts or unwanted feelings deep inside.

ARGUING WITH YOURSELF

YOU'RE A FAILURE!

NO I'M NOT!

You attempt to challenge and disprove negative thoughts.

FLIGHT

Running away or hiding from unwanted thoughts/feelings by:

HIDING/ESCAPING

You avoid situations in which you feel uncomfortable.

DISTRACTION

You focus on something else to avoid unwanted thoughts and feelings.

TAKING CHARGE

> SNAP OUT OF IT!
> STAY CALM!
> CHEER UP!

You try to force yourself to feel better.

SELF-BULLYING

> IDIOT!
> DON'T BE SO
> PATHETIC!

You beat yourself up for having these thoughts/feelings.

ZONING OUT/ NUMBING

You make yourself 'unconscious' to the thoughts/feelings.

PILLS AND DRUGS

You use medication, alcohol or drugs to escape the pain.

> BUT WHAT'S WRONG WITH THESE THINGS IF THEY HELP YOU TO COPE?

> NOTHING — IF YOU USE THEM ...

▶ IN MODERATION

▶ WHEN THEY CAN ACTUALLY WORK

▶ IF THEY DON'T STOP YOU DOING THE THINGS YOU VALUE.

For example,
DISTRACTING YOURSELF
after an argument or a
tough day can be helpful ...

I NEED SOME
TIME OUT!

... but if you spend ALL
NIGHT distracting yourself
you'll miss out on LIFE!

Any method to avoid pain, if used excessively will create
GREATER PROBLEMS:

AAH!
CHOCOLATE!

OOH AH!
DIABETES!

I'LL TAKE MY MIND
OFF THIS *EXAM
STRESS*!

Trying to BURY deep pain doesn't make it DISAPPEAR!

Avoiding painful feelings can stop you doing what you VALUE:

A simple RELAXATION
TECHNIQUE may
be enough to ease a
stressful day at WORK ...

RELAX AND
BREATHE ...

... but it won't do
much for OUTRIGHT
TERROR!

RELAX?! ARE
YOU *KIDDING*?!

AND WHILE YOU MIGHT BE
ABLE TO SIMPLY *IGNORE* A
MESSY ROOM ...

... IT'S HARD
TO IGNORE
A SINISTER
LUMP!

SO HOW DOES
THAT FIT WITH
THE *HAPPINESS*
TRAP?

THE TRAP IS THAT
TRYING TO AVOID
PAINFUL FEELINGS IS
MOSTLY *INEFFECTIVE* ...

▶ IT TAKES A LOT OF TIME AND ENERGY

▶ WE FEEL INADEQUATE WHEN THE UNWANTED
      THOUGHTS/FEELINGS COME BACK

▶ IT OFTEN HAS LONG-TERM COSTS TO WELLBEING.

... AND YOU END UP IN A LOOP WHERE THE MORE YOU TRY TO AVOID PAIN THE *WORSE* YOU FEEL!

TRY TO AVOID OR GET RID OF THEM

PAINFUL THOUGHTS AND FEELINGS

EVEN MORE PAIN

TRY EVEN HARDER TO AVOID

THIS IS KNOWN AS *'EXPERIENTIAL AVOIDANCE'*.

WHAT'S THAT MEAN?

THE ONGOING ATTEMPT TO *AVOID* OR *GET RID* OF UNWANTED THOUGHTS/FEELINGS ...

... NO MATTER THE *COST*!

BUT THE *HARDER* YOU TRY THE *WORSE* YOU FEEL, SO ROUND AND ROUND IT GOES!

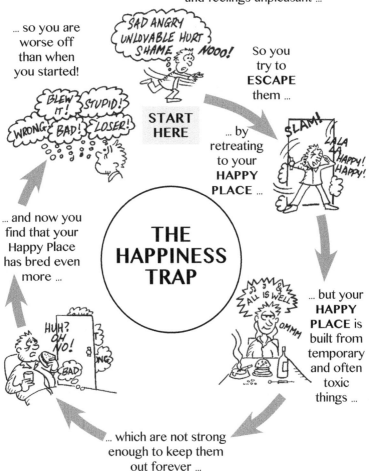

AND *VOILA!*
YOU'RE *TRAPPED!*

You find unwanted thoughts
and feelings unpleasant ...

... so you are
worse off
than when
you started!

SAD ANGRY
UNLOVABLE HURT
SHAME — NOOO!

So you
try to
ESCAPE
them ...

START
HERE

... by
retreating
to your
**HAPPY
PLACE** ...

BLEW
IT! STUPID!
WRONG! BAD! LOSER!

SLAM!
LALA
LA
HAPPY!
HAPPY!

... and now you
find that your
Happy Place
has bred even
more ...

**THE
HAPPINESS
TRAP**

ALL IS WELL
OMMM

... but your
**HAPPY
PLACE** is
built from
temporary
and often
toxic
things ...

HUH?
OH
NO!
BAD

... which are not strong
enough to keep them
out forever ...

EXERCISE

List the thoughts & feelings you'd like to get rid of. Now list every method you've used so far to avoid or get rid of them (e.g. drugs, alcohol, food, procrastination, avoiding difficult situations, etc). Did these strategies work in the long term? What was the cost?

WHAT ABOUT DOING GOOD *WORKS* AND GIVING TO OTHERS? DOESN'T THAT BRING *HAPPINESS*?

IT CAN — BUT IT WON'T BE *SATISFYING* IF YOUR MAIN AIM IS TO *AVOID* THOUGHTS AND FEELINGS SUCH AS ....

I'M A BAD FATHER!

I'M SELFISH!

NOBODY LIKES ME.

I'M NOT APPRECIATED FOR WHAT I DO!

IF I GIVE THEY'LL LIKE ME!

NEGATIVE THOUGHTS

FEELING INADEQUATE

FEARING REJECTION

DOING SOMETHING TO AVOID PAIN IS *UNFULFILLING*. MUCH BETTER TO DO IT BECAUSE IT'S *MEANINGFUL*!

Consider running through a forest. You can run through a forest to MEET YOUR LOVER.

You can run through a forest to ESCAPE A BEAR.

When we do any activity primarily to escape or avoid something unwanted, it is usually unfulfilling, because it feels like we are on the run from something, rather than doing something meaningful. Of course, we are not usually on the run from wild animals, but rather from painful thoughts and feelings.

Likewise you can go to the gym to look after and TAKE CARE OF YOUR BODY.

Or you can go to the gym to ESCAPE UNPLEASANT THOUGHTS OR FEELINGS.

You'll hear a lot of ADVICE on how to IMPROVE YOUR LIFE:

But be warned: if you start doing any of these things primarily to ESCAPE or AVOID unpleasant feelings, it probably won't be rewarding. Better to do things because they are genuinely important and meaningful, rather than to try to avoid pain.

Chapter 3

The basics of ACT

LET'S TAKE A LOOK AT *ACT* WHICH PROVIDES THE FRAMEWORK FOR YOUR JOURNEY OUT OF THE TRAP!

ACT — **ACCEPTANCE and COMMITMENT THERAPY**
— is based on two main principles: 'mindfulness' and 'values'. These principles work together to help you:

▶ **EFFECTIVELY HANDLE PAINFUL THOUGHTS AND FEELINGS**

▶ **CREATE A RICH, FULL AND MEANINGFUL LIFE.**

'Mindfulness' is a special mental state of AWARENESS and OPENNESS. Mindfulness involves three skills:

SKILL 1: DEFUSION

When you learn to defuse painful and unpleasant thoughts, self-limiting beliefs and self-criticism, they have less influence over you.

SKILL 2: EXPANSION

This means 'making room' for painful thoughts and feelings and allowing them to flow through you, without getting swept away by them.

SKILL 3: CONNECTION

This means living fully in the present instead of dwelling on the past or worrying about the future.

DEFUSION, EXPANSION AND *CONNECTION* ARE TOGETHER KNOWN AS *MINDFULNESS*.

'Values' are your heart's deepest desires for how you want to behave as a human being; what you want to STAND FOR in life.

In *ACT*, you use 'values' to give life MEANING, PURPOSE and DIRECTION.

And you translate values into COMMITTED ACTION: you do what really matters to you!

ACT is a scientifically proven method to help you build a RICHER, FULLER and more MEANINGFUL life.

Are you ready to GET MOVING? Let's go!

Chapter 4

The great storyteller

NOW WE'RE GOING TO LOOK AT HOW TO HANDLE OUR *THOUGHTS*.

WHAT *ARE* THOUGHTS EXACTLY?

THOUGHTS ARE BASICALLY *WORDS*.

WORDS?

We use words in different settings ...

WORDS ON A PAGE ARE CALLED **TEXT**:	WORDS SPOKEN OUT LOUD ARE CALLED **SPEECH**:	AND WORDS INSIDE OUR HEAD ARE CALLED **THOUGHTS**:

The quick brown fox jumps over the lazy dog.

YAKKITY YAK

BLAH BLAH BLAH

Thoughts can also be IMAGES:

WORDS　　　　**IMAGE**

BREAKFAST! I'LL HAVE TOAST AND JAM!

But please don't confuse THOUGHTS with 'FEELINGS' or 'SENSATIONS' — which we feel in the BODY.

We'll explore FEELINGS and SENSATIONS later. Let's stick with THOUGHTS for now.

THOUGHTS — TELL US ABOUT LIFE & HOW TO LIVE IT ...

... HOW WE ARE OR SHOULD BE AND WHAT TO AVOID.

DO THIS
DO THAT

LIKE THIS
DON'T LIKE THAT

What we tend to forget is that thoughts are just words which constitute our 'stories'.

These can be TRUE stories called **FACTS** ...

... or FALSE stories.

NO-ONE EVER LIKES ME!!!

IT'S MY DAY OFF!

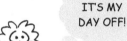

But most stories are based on how we see life according to our ...

or what we want to do with our lives:

OPINIONS
ATTITUDES
JUDGEMENTS
IDEALS
BELIEFS
MORALS

PLANS
STRATEGIES
GOALS
WISHES
VALUES

THE HUMAN MIND IS LIKE A STORYTELLING MACHINE. ALL IT WANTS IS OUR *ATTENTION*!

BLAH, BLAH, BLAH, STORY, STORY, STORY, GIVE ME YOUR ATTENTION!

BUT IF WE GET TOO *CAUGHT UP* IN THESE STORIES, IT CREATES PROBLEMS:

BAD THINGS WILL HAPPEN!

I'M NOT *GOOD ENOUGH.*

HOW *DARE* THEY?!

I *CAN'T* DO IT!

WHEN A STORY *DOMINATES* US — WHEN IT CAPTURES OUR FULL ATTENTION OR DICTATES HOW WE BEHAVE — WE REFER TO THIS AS *FUSION*.

NOW HERE'S AN *AMAZING FACT* ...

NEWS FLASH!

NO THOUGHT IS PROBLEMATIC IN AND OF ITSELF. OUR THOUGHTS ONLY BECOME PROBLEMATIC IF WE 'FUSE' WITH THEM!

REALLY?

SURE! IN A MOMENT YOU'LL SEE THAT NO MATTER HOW *NEGATIVE* A THOUGHT IS, IT'S ONLY PROBLEMATIC IF YOU *FUSE* WITH IT!

I DON'T UNDERSTAND!

THIS WILL MAKE IT CLEARER. JOT DOWN SOME OF YOUR NEGATIVE THOUGHTS ON A SHEET OF PAPER.

OKAY.

NOW HOLD THE PAPER IN FRONT OF YOUR FACE AND GET ALL ABSORBED IN THOSE WORDS.

WHILE YOU'RE ALL CAUGHT UP IN THESE THOUGHTS YOU ARE *CUT OFF* OR *DISCONNECTED* FROM THE THINGS THAT MAKE LIFE *MEANINGFUL*.

AND WHILE YOU'RE HOLDING ON TIGHTLY TO THESE *THOUGHTS*, IT'S HARD TO DO THE THINGS THAT MAKE YOUR LIFE *WORK*!

IMAGINE TRYING TO *COOK DINNER, DRIVE A CAR, CUDDLE A BABY* OR *WATCH A MOVIE* WHEN YOU'RE DOING *THIS*!

WHEN WE *FUSE* WITH OUR THOUGHTS THEY SEEM TO BE ...

▶ **THE TRUTH**	You should BELIEVE THEM!
▶ **IMPORTANT**	You should give them your FULL ATTENTION!
▶ **ORDERS**	You must OBEY them!
▶ **GREAT ADVICE**	You should do what they SUGGEST!
▶ **THREATS**	They are DANGEROUS or FRIGHTENING.

NOW TUCK THAT SHEET OF PAPER UNDER YOUR ARM ...

... AND NOTICE THAT NOW YOU CAN *CONNECT* AND *ENGAGE* WITH THE THINGS THAT MAKE LIFE *MEANINGFUL*!

WHEN YOU DO THIS WITH YOUR THOUGHTS WE CALL IT *DEFUSION*.

CAN YOU SHOW ME *HOW*?

SURE. FIRST, BRING TO MIND A *NEGATIVE SELF-JUDGEMENT* ...

I'M *USELESS*!

... NOW *FUSE* WITH IT — *BELIEVE* IT AS MUCH AS YOU CAN.

I'M *USELESS*!

53

NOW INSERT THIS PHRASE IN FRONT OF IT — 'I'M HAVING THE THOUGHT THAT ...'

I'M HAVING THE THOUGHT THAT I'M USELESS!

EXERCISE

Pick an upsetting thought, and silently repeat it, putting these words in front of it: 'I'm having the thought that ...'

Now try it again with this phrase: '*I notice I'm having the thought that ...*'

Can you feel the thought lose some of its impact?

You can use this simple defusion technique to unhook yourself from any thought, whether true or false — so please play around it.

When we defuse from our thoughts we realise they:

▶ are nothing more or less than WORDS and PICTURES

▶ may or may not be TRUE (we don't have to BELIEVE them)

▶ may or may not be IMPORTANT (we pay attention only if they're helpful)

▶ are not ORDERS (we don't have to obey!)

▶ may or may not be WISE — we don't have to follow the advice

▶ are never actual THREATS, no matter how negative.

EXERCISE

Pick a thought that bothers you, and silently sing it to the tune 'Happy Birthday'.

What happens when you do that?

Notice that you haven't tried to challenge it, avoid it, or get rid of it. But hopefully you can now see it for what it is: nothing more or less than a string of words.

The mind LOVES its STORIES! Unfortunately many of these stories are UNHELPFUL.

It's 'normal' for about 80 per cent of our thoughts to have some negative content. The trouble arises only when we FUSE with these thoughts and when we let them DOMINATE us. This feeds:

INSECURITY   **ANXIETY**   **DEPRESSION**

ANGER   **LOW SELF-ESTEEM**   **SELF-DOUBT**

Some psychological approaches advise you to:

▶ check the FACTS and correct MENTAL ERRORS

▶ make the story more POSITIVE

▶ tell yourself a better STORY

▶ DISTRACT yourself

▶ PUSH the story away

▶ DEBATE the truth of the story.

But these strategies rarely work in the long run.

NEGATIVE STORIES AREN'T THE PROBLEM! THE PROBLEM IS GETTING *CAUGHT UP IN THEM* OR LETTING THEM *DICTATE* YOUR *ACTIONS*.

Just like those tabloid stories — you can BUY INTO them ...

THAT'S *AWFUL!*

STAR DIES... OF EMBARRASSMENT

... or NOT!

BLIMEY! WHAT WILL THEY *DREAM UP* NEXT?

Trying to CHANGE, AVOID or GET RID OF a story is often INEFFECTIVE. Instead, simply name it for what it IS!

———— ————

THIS IS A *STORY*!

Try naming your own stories and see they are nothing more than WORDS.

THE 'I'M A LOSER' STORY

THE 'I'M FAT' STORY

THE 'I CAN'T COPE' STORY

THE 'I'M UNLOVABLE' STORY

Please try these defusion techniques with your own thoughts.

For example, if you have lots of thoughts about being 'not good enough' then whenever they show up, say to yourself, 'Aha! There it is again! The "Not Good Enough" story.'

If you like, you can also add, with a sense of humour, 'Thanks, mind!'

Chapter 5

True blues

ACT: WHAT'S IMPORTANT IS NOT
WHETHER OR NOT A THOUGHT IS TRUE
BUT
WHETHER OR NOT IT HELPS YOU
TO HOLD ONTO IT!

EXAMPLE 1

UNHELPFUL

HELPFUL

I'M INCOMPETENT!

I COULD ASK FOR HELP.

Does holding onto that thought when it appears IMPROVE your performance?

Belittling/ Unsettling

Expanding skills and knowledge

EXAMPLE 2

UNHELPFUL

HELPFUL

I'M A LUMP OF LARD!

I'LL GO FOR A WALK!

Does holding onto that thought when it appears make you want to LOOK AFTER yourself?

Blaming, demoralising

Making healthier choices!

EVEN IF IT'S *TRUE*!

BUT I REALLY *HAVE* BLOWN ALL MY SAVINGS!

Does getting caught in these thoughts help you COPE?

NO, I JUST FEEL MORE DEPRESSED AND THINK *WORSE* THOUGHTS!

PATHETIC!

LOSER!

NOW LET'S TAKE A LOOK AT THE SO-CALLED 'IMPOSTER SYNDROME'!

John does his job well. He's EFFICIENT and COMPETENT.

But his mind has OTHER IDEAS!

I'M A *FRAUD*. I'M JUST *LUCKY* THAT IT WORKED OUT. I'M SURE TO *BLOW IT* AND BE FOUND OUT!

With the IMPOSTER SYNDROME, John is paying more attention to his overcritical thoughts ...

... than the direct experience

YOU DON'T KNOW WHAT YOU'RE DOING!

YOU'RE SCREWING IT UP!

YEAH, *RIGHT*!

THAT'S *PERFECT* JOHN!

THANKS.

John has been 'hooked' by the 'I'm Incompetent' story. He needs to 'unhook' himself and turn his attention to what's REALLY happening.

EXERCISES

1. NOT TAKING A THOUGHT SERIOUSLY

Imagine the thought on a computer screen.

Play around with the font and the colour.

2. THANKING YOUR MIND

When the same old stories come up,

MY LIFE'S HOPELESS.

say them to yourself with a sense of humour!

AHA! HERE IT IS AGAIN! THE 'MY LIFE'S HOPELESS' STORY!

IS THAT *RIGHT*? THANKS FOR SHARING!

OR simply —

THANKS MIND!

3. SILLY VOICES

Pick a recurring self-judgement.

I'M STUPID!

Silently say it to yourself in the voice of a cartoon or movie character.

I'M STHTOOPID!

4. KIDS COMIC BOOK

I CAN'T DO IT!

Imagine your thought inside a thought bubble in a comic book.

SUPAGUY
I CAN'T DO IT?

Again, notice that you have not tried to avoid or change the thought, you've just seen it for what it is — WORDS.

BUT I HAVE *TERMINAL CANCER*! IF I HAVE A THOUGHT THAT I'LL BE DEAD SOON, THAT'S BOTH *TRUE* AND *SERIOUS*!

YES, BUT IS IT *HELPFUL* TO GET ENTANGLED IN THOSE THOUGHTS? DO YOU WANT TO SPEND THE TIME YOU HAVE LEFT STUCK INSIDE YOUR THOUGHTS OR DOING THINGS THAT *MATTER*?

I'M SORRY BUT I CAN'T DO THE SILLY VOICES FOR THIS. IT'S TOO *PAINFUL*!

That's fine; pick another technique that works for you.

HOW LONG DO I HAVE TO DO THESE?

Until you are able to defuse your thoughts quickly.

DEFUSION GUIDELINES

▶ See the thoughts for what they are — nothing more or less than WORDS.

▶ Don't EXPECT anything. Just observe what happens.

▶ The thoughts may go or not. The technique may work sometimes but not at others.

▶ You're HUMAN — your thoughts will snare you again. But now you know how you can quickly unhook yourself.

▶ Like any skill, the more you practise the better you get.

NO TECHNIQUE IS *FOOLPROOF*. EVEN DEFUSION HAS ITS STICKING POINTS — LET'S EXAMINE AND UNSTICK THEM.

Chapter 6

Troubleshooting defusion

I TRIED DEFUSION AND IT DOESN'T *WORK*.

YOU MEAN YOU STAYED *ENTANGLED* IN THE STORY?

NO. I UNHOOKED MYSELF BUT I STILL FELT *ANXIOUS*!

BUT DEFUSION IS NOT A WAY TO *CONTROL* YOUR FEELINGS!

THE PURPOSE OF DEFUSION IS ...

... to see your thoughts as words and unhook yourself — so you can do the things that matter and engage in them fully.

BUT I DON'T *LIKE* FEELING ANXIOUS!

OF *COURSE*! NOBODY DOES!

But the more you struggle with painful feelings, the bigger they get! Later in the book we'll show you a new way to handle them!

HMPH! I DID THAT DEFUSION TECHNIQUE BUT THE THOUGHTS DIDN'T *GO AWAY.*

SOMETIMES THEY GO, SOMETIMES THEY STAY. WE'RE NOT TRYING TO GET *RID* OF THE THOUGHTS — JUST TO *UNHOOK* OURSELVES.

BUT SHOULDN'T I TRY TO THINK MORE *POSITIVELY*?

THE ISSUE IS NOT WHETHER YOUR THOUGHTS ARE *POSITIVE* OR *NEGATIVE.* THE QUESTION IS THIS ...

IF I LET THIS THOUGHT GUIDE WHAT I DO, WILL IT HELP ME CREATE THE LIFE I WANT?

BUT POSITIVE THOUGHTS ARE ALWAYS *HELPFUL,* AREN'T THEY?

WELL, A DRUNK DRIVER MAY THINK HE'S COMPETENT TO DRIVE — THAT *IS* A POSITIVE THOUGHT, BUT IS IT *HELPFUL?*

BUT NEGATIVE THOUGHTS ARE *UNHELPFUL* RIGHT?

NOT NECESSARILY! IF A NEGATIVE THOUGHT LEADS TO *POSITIVE* ACTION, IT CAN BE *HELPFUL.*

I MIGHT SCREW UP THE TEST!

I'D BETTER GO DO SOME PREPARATION!

Negative thoughts are not the ENEMY! They are just WORDS and PICTURES floating through your mind. Fight them and you'll be fighting YOURSELF.

SO IS *FUSION* EVER *HELPFUL?*

IT CAN BE!

Planning your future, mentally rehearsing your actions, getting lost in a book can all be HELPFUL types of FUSION.

So when a thought appears, if it's helpful, USE it and if not, DEFUSE it.

Increase your AWARENESS of when and where you fuse, and the sorts of thoughts you tend to fuse with. The aim is to get better at catching yourself doing it, so you can then consciously choose how to act on those thoughts.

And like learning any new skill you'll need to PRACTISE till it becomes more natural to you. Pick ONE or TWO defusion techniques and practise them at every opportunity. AT LEAST 10 times a day but the more the better!

So if at this point your mind says:

IDIOT!

THEN DEFUSE!

STUPID THING TO SAY!

THEN DEFUSE!

MY LIFE SUCKS!

THEN DEFUSE!

IT'S ALL TOO HARD. I CAN'T BE BOTHERED.

And if you're now thinking ...

THANKS MIND!

DEFUSE FROM THAT TOO!

There are TWO PARTS to your MIND:

THE THINKING SELF
is responsible for:
    THINKING
    PLANNING
    JUDGING
    COMPARING
    CREATING
    VISUALISING
    IMAGINING
    ANALYSING

THE OBSERVING SELF
is responsible for:
    ATTENTION
    AWARENESS
    CONSCIOUSNESS
    NOTICING
    OBSERVING

WHEN PEOPLE USE THE WORD 'MIND' THEY USUALLY MEAN THE *THINKING SELF.*

Life is like a STAGE SHOW and on that stage are all your THOUGHTS and FEELINGS and everything you can SEE, HEAR, TOUCH, TASTE and SMELL.

The OBSERVING SELF is the part of you that can step back and watch the show.

PRESENTING

Thoughts
Feelings
Touch
Taste
Sight
Hearing
Smell!

Life

The OBSERVING SELF can zoom in and take in the DETAILS or zoom out and take in the WHOLE SHOW — and the show CONTINUALLY CHANGES.

EXERCISE

For 60 SECONDS close your eyes and notice what THOUGHTS appear ...

The THINKING SELF creates the thoughts. The OBSERVING SELF notices the thoughts.

Remember — because of the way it evolved, our mind is a bit like RADIO DOOM AND GLOOM:

And you can't turn it off! In fact, the HARDER you try, the LOUDER it gets!

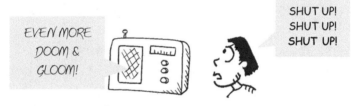

So if it's broadcasting a HELPFUL story, tune in, and let it guide your actions.

But if it's broadcasting something unhelpful, just let it chatter away in the BACKGROUND.

This doesn't mean you get into a debate with the radio ...

... or try to IGNORE it ...

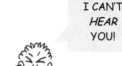

HEY! I'M *TALKIN'* TO YOU!

I CAN'T *HEAR* YOU!

... you just let it chatter away and ENGAGE in what you're doing.

EXERCISE

Take 10 SLOW, DEEP BREATHS.
Focus fully on the BREATH
and the sensations of BREATHING.

Now let your thoughts
come and go like
PASSING CARS.
Acknowledge them but
stay focused on your
BREATHING.

HMM ...THERE *GO MY THOUGHTS.*

If a thought SNAGS you, gently UNHOOK yourself and REFOCUS on your breathing.

BY PRACTISING THIS TECHNIQUE YOU LEARN HOW TO:

▶ let thoughts come and go

▶ recognise when you've become hooked on a thought

▶ unhook and refocus.

▶ Take what comes — let go of any expectations. If it relaxes you, great but that's a bonus, not the aim.

▶ It doesn't matter how often you get 'hooked'. Regular unhooking improves your skills.

▶ It's best to practise this for 5–10 minutes, two to three times a day.

NOW REMEMBER, THOUGHTS CAN BE *WORDS* OR *IMAGES*.

We've all conjured up FRIGHTENING IMAGES in our heads ...

and fusing with these images can stop us doing what we VALUE.

NO WAY I'M GETTING ON A *PLANE*!

When we FUSE with these images they seem very REAL or IMPORTANT or SCARY but we can DEFUSE from images, too. Try the following exercises:

EXERCISES

Bring to mind an unpleasant image. Notice how it affects you.

Imagine the image on a TV SCREEN.

Now play around with it — SLOW MOTION, BACKWARDS or change to BLACK AND WHITE.

See? It's just a PICTURE!

Now add a HUMOROUS TITLE or a SILLY VOICEOVER, or ODD MUSIC.

TERROR IN SUBURBIA

(IN 3D)

And here in her natural habitat, we see Jenny ...

DUM DUM DA DA!

(Tchaikovsky's 1812 overture)

Or try shifting the LOCATION of the troublesome image. Mentally picture it on a ...

T SHIRT **CANVAS** **COMIC** **POSTAGE STAMP**

If the mental image is still pushing you around, run through these exercises every day till it loosens its grip. You can also adapt previous defusion techniques:

NAMING THE STORY

NAMING THE PICTURE

or use ...

Here's one final technique (great for moving images).

Change your video clip ...

... to a different GENRE!

CARTOON   **WESTERN**   **SCI FI**   **SOAP OPERA**

THE AIM IS TO *UNHOOK* — NOT TO GET *RID* OF THEM!

WHY?

BECAUSE THEY WILL COME BACK AGAIN AND AGAIN AND FIGHTING THEM IS *HARD WORK*!

REMEMBER — SOMETIMES THESE TECHNIQUES WILL UNHOOK YOU AND SOMETIMES NOT. TAKE WHAT COMES.

Chapter 7

Demons in the boat

Imagine you are in a boat far out to SEA ...

... and below deck are a bunch of demons which are EMOTIONS, THOUGHTS, FEELINGS and URGES.

If you keep DRIFTING AIMLESSLY they stay below, but as you near land they clamber on deck and OVERWHELM you.

So you make a DEAL.

I'LL KEEP DRIFTING IF YOU STAY BELOW.

OKAY.

But drifting is not FUN.

ANXIOUS BORED LONELY

I *HATE* THIS!

Besides, other ships are happily landing. Why not YOURS?

But if you try to land, the demons will RESURFACE! WHAT TO DO?

You could try to throw the demons OVERBOARD ...

... but then no-one would be steering and you might SINK.

And besides, there are TOO MANY to fight off.

But take a GOOD LOOK at those demons in BROAD DAYLIGHT and you'll discover that they're noisy and ugly but they can't actually HARM you.

GROWL!
GRUMP!

And once you get used to them they're not really THAT scary.

And you'll see they're much SMALLER than you thought!

They may never be cute and cuddly but they no longer have POWER over you.

YOU CAN'T CONTROL ME!

So now you can head to shore and do the things you LIKE!

Your demons love to pop up when you try new things but they can't STOP you!

Ask yourself:

▶ How would I act differently if my 'demons' were no longer a problem?

▶ What activities would I start (or continue)?

▶ What would I do, if fear wasn't a barrier?

▶ What would I stand for, if fear couldn't stop me?

(Are troublesome thoughts or images popping up for you? If so, you know how to defuse!)

Now let's explore the scariest demons of all — **PAINFUL EMOTIONS**.

SO WHAT *ARE* EMOTIONS?

WELL SCIENTIFICALLY SPEAKING THEY:

▶ originate in the mid brain

▶ involve complex changes in your body.

These changes prepare us for action and lead to a TENDENCY to act in a certain way.

HERE'S SOMEONE EXPERIENCING A STRONG EMOTION — LIKE ANXIETY.

PHYSICAL SENSATIONS

Fast shallow breathing

Increased heart rate

Sweating

Churning stomach

Urge to run

ACTION TENDENCY

Talk rapidly

Fidget

Pace up and down

NOTICE THE USE OF THE WORD *TENDENCY* WHICH MEANS AN *INCLINATION*!

SO WE *TEND* TO BUT WE DON'T *HAVE* TO?

YES — IF YOU'RE RUNNING LATE, YOU MAY *TEND* TO WANT TO SPEED BUT *CHOOSE* NOT TO.

WHOA! TAKE IT *EASY*!

Emotions are made up of: WORDS and IMAGES in your head and SENSATIONS and FEELINGS in your body.

I'M SCARED THIS MIGHT GO WRONG.

SO DO OUR EMOTIONS CONTROL OUR *BEHAVIOUR*?

IN A WORD — *NO*!

You can feel ANGRY but act CALM.

You may have a TENDENCY to shout or lash out.

But you don't HAVE TO. You can choose OTHERWISE.

You may have felt fear ... and a TENDENCY to run ...

... but you chose NOT TO.

But though you may not have direct control over your FEELINGS ...

... you can directly control your ACTIONS.

DON'T RUN! BACK AWAY SLOWLY!

THE IDEA THAT EMOTIONS CONTROL ACTIONS IS A POWERFUL *ILLUSION*!

When you feel strong emotions it may SEEM as though the emotion is causing your actions.

But with practice, you can control how you act, even when feeling very strong emotions.

Even when you're FURIOUS you can still ...

▶ stand still
▶ speak softly
▶ drink water
▶ go to the toilet.

Emotions are like the weather — ever changing and always present.

MILD PLEASANT   INTENSE UNPLEASANT

PREDICTABLE

Some people are very in touch with and can express their feelings ...

I FEEL ANXIOUS AND AGITATED.

UNEXPECTED

... while others are more disconnected and have difficulty accessing their feelings.

I DUNNO, I FEEL OKAY I GUESS.

There are THREE PHASES in the creation of an emotion:

1 A significant event occurs either **INTERNALLY (e.g. a thought)**

or **EXTERNALLY**

and your brain registers this as IMPORTANT ...

2 ... and does an EVALUATION **GOOD? BAD?**

... and prepares you for APPROPRIATE ACTION. **STAY? GO?**

3 The mind then tells a STORY about the experience ...

FRUSTRATING?
JOYOUS?
SAD?
EXCITING?
GUILTY?

THIS IS *FUN*!

THIS IS *AWFUL*!

... which others may or may not SHARE.

NOTE THAT AT PHASE 2 YOU MIGHT EXPERIENCE A *FIGHT OR FLIGHT* RESPONSE!

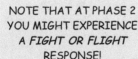

WHAT'S THAT?

IT'S THE SAME ANCESTRAL
'DON'T GET KILLED' MESSAGE ...

To save yourself
you either stand
and FIGHT the
woolly mammoth ...

... or take FLIGHT!

Our minds have evolved to look for danger
EVERYWHERE ...

A MOODY SPOUSE	A BIG MORTGAGE	A CONTROLLING BOSS	OR EVEN A FRIGHTENING THOUGHT!

The fight or flight response triggers unpleasant or
'negative' feelings.

GUILT

FEAR

However, if our brain registers the event as 'good' then
pleasant 'positive' feelings are triggered.

JOY

PLEASURE

DELIGHT

But 'NEGATIVE' and
'POSITIVE' are just
LABELS for what are
simply FEELINGS.

WELL I'D STILL PREFER THE *POSITIVE* ONES!

OF *COURSE*! BUT MAKING THAT PREFERENCE INTO AN 'ABSOLUTE MUST CREATES PROBLEMS.

SO LET'S LOOK AT A NEW WAY TO HANDLE PAINFUL FEELINGS.

Chapter 8

Drop the struggle

Most of us readily buy into STORIES about painful emotions such as:

ANGER
GUILT
SHAME
FEAR
EMBARRASSMENT
AND ANXIETY
ARE 'NEGATIVE'
EMOTIONS.

WHICH
ARE *BAD*
DANGEROUS
IRRATIONAL
AND A SIGN OF
WEAKNESS.

AND SHOW
I *HAVE*
PSYCHOLOGICAL
DEFECTS.

THEY'LL
DAMAGE MY
HEALTH.

PEOPLE SHOULD
HIDE THEIR
FEELINGS.

THEY SHOW
A LACK OF
CONTROL.

I MUST
KEEP MY
EMOTIONS
UNDER
CONTROL.

WOMEN
SHOULDN'T
GET *ANGRY.*

MEN
SHOULDN'T
FEEL *AFRAID.*

IF I DON'T CONTROL MY FEELINGS SOMETHING *BAD* WILL HAPPEN!

NEGATIVE EMOTION MEANS THERE'S SOMETHING *WRONG* WITH MY LIFE.

Your outlook on expressing emotion is heavily influenced by your CHILDHOOD PROGRAMMING. Negative emotions may have been ...

SUPPRESSED

CHEER UP! ITS ONLY *A DOLL*!

FOR GOODNESS SAKE *'BE A MAN'*!

IF ALLOWED, COULD HAVE BEEN FRIGHTENING

GET IT OFF YOUR *CHEST*!

EXERCISE

Take note of your childhood programming about EMOTIONS.

1. What messages were you given?
2. Which emotions were you told were desirable or undesirable?
3. What were you told about the best way to handle emotions?
4. What emotions did your family freely express? Suppress? Frown upon? Hide?
5. With which emotions were your family comfortable? Uncomfortable?
6. How did the adults handle their own emotions?
7. How did they react to your emotions?
8. What did you learn from observing this as you grew?
9. What ideas do you still retain from your programming?

JUDGING OUR EMOTIONS

We tend to judge emotions according to how they FEEL.

BAD   GOOD

Unpleasant
Don't want

Pleasant
Want more

ACT – let go of judging and see them as what they are:

▶ **Constantly changing SENSATIONS moving through your body.**

▶ **No emotion is 'GOOD' or 'BAD'.**

▶ **An emotion may be PAINFUL or PLEASANT but if we FUSE with the thought that it's BAD, we will struggle with it and make it WORSE.**

MY FAMILY DIDN'T OPENLY EXPRESS LOVE AND AFFECTION. I FEEL *UNCOMFORTABLE* DOING SO.

BUT DOES THAT MAKE THESE FEELINGS *BAD*?

WELL I *HATE* FEELING ANXIOUS!

OF *COURSE*! IT'S UNPLEASANT! *NO-ONE* ENJOYS IT!

Your mind WILL judge your feelings but you can DEFUSE from these judgements. Here are some examples of DEFUSION TECHNIQUES you can use:

I CAN'T STAND THIS FEELING!

I'M HAVING A THOUGHT THAT I CAN'T STAND THIS FEELING.

THIS IS *AWFUL*!

I'M *NOTICING THE JUDGEMENT* THAT THIS ANXIETY IS AWFUL.

Judging ADDS to emotional discomfort and so does ...

REVIEWING

WHY AM I FEELING LIKE THIS?

Reviewing all your PROBLEMS creates the illusion that your life is nothing BUT problems.

REHASHING

WHAT HAVE I DONE TO *DESERVE* THIS?

Rehashing all your 'CRIMES' to explain this 'PUNISHMENT' leads to SELF-BLAME.

SEARCHING

WHY AM I LIKE THIS?

Searching your life history for someone to BLAME can lead to anger, resentment and hopelessness.

WHAT'S *WRONG* WITH ME?

This is another review of all your FAULTS and FLAWS.

I CAN'T HANDLE IT.

Your mind is feeding you a DISEMPOWERING STORY.

I SHOULDN'T FEEL LIKE THIS!

This is the mind ARGUING with itself.

I WISH I DIDN'T FEEL LIKE THIS.

Wishing it wasn't like this doesn't change the REALITY.

ASK YOURSELF: IF I HOLD ONTO THESE THOUGHTS, IS THAT *HELPFUL*? DO THEY MAKE IT *EASIER* OR *HARDER* TO HANDLE THE PAIN?

When we feel painful feelings we naturally do what we can to AVOID or GET RID OF them.

But often the things that give us RELIEF in the SHORT TERM ... ... make our life WORSE in the LONG TERM.

SO HOW DO WE *COPE* WITH PAINFUL FEELINGS?

WE LEARN A SKILL CALLED 'EXPANSION'.

In order to understand EXPANSION look at some words that describe FEELING BAD:

TENSION — being stretched or stressed

STRESS — subject to strain or pressure

STRAIN — to shock beyond proper limits.

In other words — these terms describe being pulled apart
or STRETCHED BEYOND OUR LIMITS.

SORROW   **PAIN**

GUILT   **GRIEF**

These words imply
that the emotions are
simply too BIG for
us to accommodate
— that we don't have
'enough room' for
them.

NOW LET'S LOOK AT
WHAT WE MEAN BY
EXPANSION:

EXPAND: spread
unfold
develop.

BUT IF I OPEN UP TO
MY FEELINGS THEY'LL
TAKE OVER AND I'LL
LOSE CONTROL!

THAT'S JUST YOUR
MIND TELLING YOU
SCARY STORIES!
THANK IT AND MAKE
ROOM FOR OTHER
POSSIBILITIES.

BEFORE WE
GO ANY
FURTHER,
LET'S REVISIT
A VERY
HELPFUL IDEA.

OH?
WHAT
IS IT?

REMEMBER THE TWO PARTS TO YOUR MIND, THE THINKING SELF AND OBSERVING SELF?

AH YES! CAN YOU REMIND ME AGAIN?

CERTAINLY ...

The **THINKING SELF** is
THOUGHTS
MOVEMENTS
IMAGES
MEMORIES

The **OBSERVING SELF** is
AWARENESS
ATTENTION
FOCUS

EXERCISE

Use your OBSERVING SELF to notice what is happening in your body and let your THOUGHTS come and go like a radio in the background.

Is your BREATHING SHALLOW? DEEP? FAST? SLOW?

How does your MOUTH feel? WARM? COOL? WET? DRY?

Position of ARMS?

Is there any tension in your NECK or SHOULDERS?

Do you feel HOT or COLD? WHERE do you feel this?

Is your SPINE STRAIGHT or BENT?

Position of LEGS?

How are your FEET placed?

Scan your whole body and notice any TENSION, PAIN or DISCOMFORT.

Now notice any PLEASANT or COMFORTABLE sensations.

Do you feel like SHIFTING? Shift and notice how it feels.

Do you feel any urge to EAT, SLEEP, SCRATCH, STRETCH?

NOTICING your body is different to THINKING about it.

THINKING SELF gives the 'commentary'.

WHAT'S THE *POINT* OF THIS?

I HOPE I'M DOING IT *RIGHT*.

OBSERVING SELF just notices the sensations.

And sometimes, for brief moments when you are observing the THINKING SELF shuts up!

In EXPANSION we sidestep our thoughts and connect with our emotions through the OBSERVING SELF. In doing so, we experience emotions as they are rather than as the THINKING SELF says they are i.e. we NOTICE rather than THINK.

When there is traffic outside your window you don't leap up to check every car! Likewise. you don't have to respond to every THOUGHT!

But if a 'screeching tyre' distracts you, simply REFOCUS.

IN EXPANSION YOU LET THOUGHTS *COME AND GO* IN THE BACKGROUND AND KEEP YOUR *ATTENTION* ON THE *SENSATIONS* IN YOUR *BODY*.

REMEMBER:

▶ Emotions arise from PHYSICAL CHANGES in the body.

▶ Focus on their PHYSICAL SENSATIONS.

EXPANSION WITH PAINFUL EMOTIONS: 3 steps

1 **OBSERVE** Scan your body for uncomfortable feelings.

Are they STILL
or MOVING?

How DEEP
do they go?

Where are they
STRONGEST?
WEAKEST?

Where do they
START and END?

Find the sensation
that bothers you
most and observe
it with CURIOSITY
and OPENNESS.

2 **BREATHE**

SLOW, DEEP
BREATHS

Breathe directly
INTO and AROUND
sensations and make
ROOM for them.

It's as if you open
up and expand
AROUND the feelings.

3 **ALLOW**

THANKS
MIND!

ALLOW the
sensations to be
there even if you
don't LIKE them.

Say 'Thanks
mind' to any
RESISTANCE.

Simply
acknowledge
any unhelpful
thoughts.

Don't try to GET RID OF the sensation or ALTER it. The goal is to see it as it is, and make PEACE with it. Focus on the sensation until you DROP THE STRUGGLE WITH IT. Then move onto another sensation until you are no longer fighting them.

By being WILLING to feel them they'll have less impact and influence over you.

BUT ISN'T THAT *MASOCHISTIC?*

ONLY IF IT SERVES NO *GOOD PURPOSE*!

SO WHAT'S THE *GOOD PURPOSE?*

IMPROVING YOUR *HEALTH* AND TO LEARN VALUABLE SKILLS TO *TRANSFORM YOUR LIFE*!

OKAY, I'LL *GIVE IT A GO*!

GOOD! SO BRING TO MIND SOMETHING THAT *DISTRESSES* YOU, GET IN TOUCH WITH A *PAINFUL FEELING*, AND PRACTISE THE 3 STEPS OF EXPANSION.

EXERCISE

Please practise the 3-step exercise described above, for 3 to 5 minutes, two or three times a day.

In the next chapter, we'll look at any difficulties you may encounter.

Chapter 9

Troubleshooting expansion

The concept of EXPANSION is simple but it's not EASY!
But like any meaningful challenge it's worth the effort.
Let's explore some of the difficulties you may encounter
in the beginning and troubleshoot them.

I TRIED MAKING
ROOM FOR THE
FEELINGS BUT
THEY WERE TOO
OVERWHELMING!

DON'T TRY TO TAKE
ON TOO MUCH.
JUST DO *ONE*
SENSATION FIRST
THEN THE NEXT.

WOW! THE
FEELINGS
DISAPPEARED!

ENJOY THAT WHEN
IT HAPPENS — BUT
REMEMBER, IT'S A *BONUS*,
NOT THE MAIN AIM.

I MADE *ROOM*
BUT THE
FEELINGS WERE
STILL THERE!

THEY WILL COME
AND STAY AND
GO IN THEIR
OWN GOOD TIME.

OKAY, I'VE MADE ROOM FOR MY FEELINGS, *NOW WHAT*?

NOW IT'S TIME TO TAKE EFFECTIVE ACTION IN LINE WITH YOUR *VALUES*.

WHY DO YOU KEEP COMING BACK TO *ACTION* AND *VALUES*?

TO CREATE A *RICH* AND *FULL* LIFE WE NEED TO ACT ON OUR VALUES (AS YOU'LL SEE LATER IN THIS BOOK).

IS SLOW, DEEP BREATHING ESSENTIAL?

NO, BUT IT'S HELPFUL. *OBSERVING* AND *ALLOWING* ARE KEY, THOUGH.

BUT WHEN I'M UPSET I JUST *GO NUMB*!

MAKE *ROOM* FOR YOUR NUMBNESS FIRST. YOU MAY FIND OTHER FEELINGS FOLLOW.

HOW CAN I DO THIS EXERCISE IF I'M AT WORK OR SOMEWHERE *PUBLIC*?

DO IT *QUICKLY*! TAKE A DEEP BREATH AND MAKE ROOM FOR THE FEELING. THEN ENGAGE IN THE TASK AT HAND.

CAN THE *THINKING SELF* HELP EXPANSION?

YES — WITH *SELF-TALK* AND *IMAGERY*.

EXPANSION SELF-TALK

I DON'T *LIKE* THIS FEELING BUT I HAVE *ROOM* FOR IT.

IT'S UNPLEASANT BUT I *ACCEPT* IT.

I'M HAVING THE *FEELING* OF ...

I DON'T *LIKE* IT OR *WANT* IT BUT I WON'T *FIGHT* IT.

EXPANSION IMAGERY

Scan for unpleasant feelings. Visualise the sensation as an object.

What size?
Shape?
Colour?
Texture?
Fixed?
Shifting?

Now breathe into it and make room for it.

HOW MUCH *PRACTICE* DO I NEED TO DO?

AT LEAST *3 TIMES A DAY*, BUT THE MORE THE *BETTER*! TRAINING MAKES YOU SKILFUL.

BUT ISN'T IT *UNHEALTHY* TO KEEP FOCUSING ON UNPLEASANT FEELINGS?

YES, IF YOU ARE *CONSTANTLY DWELLING* ON THEM BUT NOT IF YOU ARE LEARNING *EXPANSION SKILLS*.

The aim is to let your feelings come and stay and go without a STRUGGLE. Focus on them ONLY to practise expansion. Otherwise, focus on doing what you VALUE.

Chapter 10

Great connections

HELLO?
ANYONE
HOME?

We've all 'drifted off' at times.

The **THINKING SELF** has one job only: to generate thoughts. But sometimes these thoughts can be DISTRACTING.

This is how we habitually go through most of our lives!

I DON'T REMEMBER HALF THE JOURNEY!

How much do you give your FULL ATTENTION to:

I MUST HAVE READ THIS PAGE *SIX TIMES*!

EATING?

WORKING?

READING?

There are times when being absorbed in our thoughts ASSISTS what we are doing ...

HMM, HOW CAN I *SOLVE* THIS?

But too often it DOESN'T.

I'VE GOT NOTHING TO SAY! HE THINKS I'M *BORING*!

MUST DO MY TAXES!

We become DISCONNECTED. This is where CONNECTION comes in.

IT'S BEING FULLY PRESENT AND AWAKE IN THE *HERE* AND *NOW* AND BEING *CURIOUS* ABOUT AND OPEN TO WHATEVER IS HAPPENING.

WHAT'S THAT?

WHY IS THIS *IMPORTANT*?

SO YOU CAN ENGAGE *FULLY* IN LIFE.

TO FULLY APPRECIATE YOUR LIFE YOU NEED TO GIVE IT YOUR ATTENTION!

YOU COULD BE EATING THE MOST BEAUTIFUL MEAL OF YOUR LIFE BUT IF YOU'RE LOST IN YOUR THOUGHTS YOU'LL HARDLY EVEN *TASTE* IT.

PRESENT

PAST

I HOPE I DON'T LOOK *GREEDY*!

WORK WAS *HELL* TODAY.

FUTURE

WILL I GET THAT REPORT IN ON *TIME*?

As LEO TOLSTOY put it ...

THERE IS ONLY ONE TIME THAT IS IMPORTANT: **NOW!**

We can only ever take action here and now, and to take effective and valuable action we need to be fully present.

CONNECTION is:

▶ waking up

▶ noticing what's happening

▶ appreciating the fullness of every moment.

This comes NATURALLY in life's wonderful moments, but it's hard to do when life is DIFFICULT or PAINFUL!

Here's a comparison between **FUSION** and **CONNECTION**:

FUSION	CONNECTION	FUSION	CONNECTION
DISTRACTED	ENGAGED	JUDGEMENTAL	DEFUSED FROM JUDGEMENTS

WHAT'S OVER *THERE?*

This should be better   I shouldn't be like this

THIS IS WRONG!

CONNECTION EXERCISES

GUIDELINES

If thoughts or feelings distract you:

- let them come and go
- bring back your attention when it wanders (and it will!)
- silently say 'Thanks Mind'.

1. Connection with ENVIRONMENT — 30 seconds

Put the book down and notice your SURROUNDINGS.

Use all your senses. Notice five things that you can:

HEAR
SEE
FEEL.

2. Awareness of your BODY — 30 seconds

Notice the POSITION of your whole BODY.

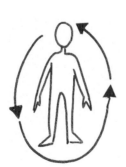

Do an internal scan and notice what you feel in EVERY PART.

3. Awareness of BREATH — 30 seconds

Connect with
your BREATHING.

Notice the FLOW
in and out.
Notice what your
body does with
the breath.

4. Awareness of SOUNDS — 30 seconds

What do
you HEAR?

SO, WHAT DID
YOU NOTICE?

I DIDN'T
REALISE
THERE WAS SO
MUCH GOING
ON THAT I'D
MISSED!

WE ARE
SO EASILY
DISCONNECTED
AREN'T WE?

When we fuse with the stories our mind tells us, it keeps us DISCONNECTED from all that life offers.

The more we get caught up in unpleasant THOUGHTS and FEELINGS, the more we are cut off from what's ACTUALLY happening and our chance to engage with what we DO want.

We can get hooked by DOOM and GLOOM about the FUTURE:

We can get hooked by DOOM and GLOOM about the PAST:

IT MIGHT BE AWFUL!

I LOST EVERYTHING!

THERE'S NO POINT!

It's hard to enjoy what you're doing if you're not connected with it, if you're LOST IN THOUGHTS!

But the REVERSE is also true!

I'M REALLY INTO THIS!

So CONNECTION is an important skill for getting the MOST out of life.

EXERCISE: CONNECT WITH PLEASANT ACTIVITIES

Practise connection with at least one pleasant activity each day.

EXERCISE: CONNECTION WITH A USEFUL CHORE

Pick a chore you don't like and practise connection.

- Have no EXPECTATIONS.
- Just NOTICE what you do.
- Open your SENSES to what's happening.

- If you feel boredom or frustration MAKE ROOM for it.
- If your attention wanders, thank your mind and REFOCUS.

EXERCISE: CONNECTION WITH A TASK YOU'VE BEEN AVOIDING

Pick a task you've been putting off.

Set aside 20 minutes and make a start on it with connection.

After 20 minutes you are free to stop or continue.

Do 20 minutes a day till the task is completed.

Practising connection is like building MUSCLES to strengthen your ability to handle change and move on with your life.

And important changes usually involve DISCOMFORT.

NEW CAREER ➡ Starting from scratch **ASKING SOMEONE OUT** ➡ Possible rejection

AVOIDANCE =
NO CHANGE/STUCK

CONNECTION =
MOVEMENT/IMPROVEMENT

AREN'T THE REWARDS *WORTH IT?*

You can CONNECT, DEFUSE and EXPAND ... or NOT! The choice is yours.

Another word that describes a process of DEFUSION, EXPANSION and CONNECTION is 'MINDFULNESS'.

This is not about having a 'FULL MIND'!

The *ACT* definition of MINDFULNESS would be:

▶ paying attention with openness and curiosity

▶ making room for whatever thoughts and feelings arise

▶ engaging fully in your here-and-now experience.

EXERCISE: MINDFUL BREATHING

Take six slow deep breaths. After a full out breath, breathe in gently. (If you're doing it right, your tummy will expand.) Practise connection: notice your breath flowing in and out!

> *MINDFUL BREATHING* IS A GOOD WAY TO PRACTISE YOUR MINDFULNESS SKILLS.

What did you notice?

> MY TENSION EASED.

> MINE DIDN'T!

> I STARTED 'LETTING GO'.

> I DIDN'T!

> I CONNECTED WITH MY BODY.

> I DIDN'T!

> MY MIND WENT QUIET.

> MINE DIDN'T!

> IF YOU DIDN'T FIND THE EXERCISE HELPFUL, PLEASE DO PERSIST. IF YOU PRACTISE IT FIVE TIMES A DAY FOR TWO WEEKS, YOU SHOULD START TO NOTICE THE BENEFITS.

MINDFUL BREATHING can connect you with the HERE and NOW.

THREE EXERCISES

Take 6 breaths again but for the first three focus on the BREATHING itself.

**CHEST
ABDOMEN**

For the next three expand your focus to include your SURROUNDINGS.

**CHEST
ABDOMEN**

What did you NOTICE?

Now do 9 breaths

First three: Focus on BREATHING.

Next three: Focus on BREATHING and THOUGHTS.

Last three: Focus on BREATHING and what you FEEL in your BODY.

This variation rapidly increases self-awareness, helps you accept thoughts and feelings and gather your wits.

Now do 12 breaths

First three: Focus on BREATHING only.

Second three: Focus on BREATHING and THOUGHTS.

Third three: Focus on BREATHING and THOUGHTS and BODY.

Final three: A broad focus on BREATHING and THOUGHTS and BODY and the WORLD AROUND YOU.

NOTE: MINDFUL BREATHING IS NOT A *RELAXATION TECHNIQUE* OR A WAY TO *AVOID FEELINGS*. IT'S AN ANCHOR, TO HOLD YOU STEADY IN THE MIDST OF AN EMOTIONAL STORM.

REMEMBER — EVEN <u>ONE</u> SLOW, DEEP BREATH CAN HELP TO ANCHOR YOU UNTIL THE STORM PASSES.

Fancy a CHALLENGE?

EXERCISE

(Allow 10 minutes, once or twice a day.)

Sit or lie comfortably.

Let your thoughts come and go.

Focus on your breath for 6 minutes.

When your attention wanders, refocus.

For the next 3 minutes focus attention on your body, and its feelings and sensations.

For the final minute open your eyes and take in the room around you.

Regular practice will bring noticeable PHYSICAL and PSYCHOLOGICAL benefits.

Chapter 11

You're not who you think you are

What do you most DISLIKE about yourself?

These are only a few of the most common responses. The range is infinite but there is one basic theme:

I'M NOT GOOD ENOUGH AS I AM!

No matter how hard we try or what we achieve, our THINKING SELF always finds FAULT with us.

YOU MIGHT TELL YOURSELF *GOOD THINGS* ABOUT YOURSELF ...

I'M DOING WELL AT MY JOB. I EAT WELL, EXERCISE, I'M GENEROUS. THEREFORE I'M A *GOOD PERSON.*

AND IF YOU CAN TRULY *BELIEVE* THAT YOU ARE A GOOD PERSON YOU WILL FEEL GOOD.

BUT ALL TOO OFTEN YOU FIND YOURSELF HAVING TO *PROVE* OR *JUSTIFY* THIS POSITION ...

I'M GOOD ... ... AREN'T I?

... OR HAVING TO *DISPUTE* THE 'NOT GOOD ENOUGH' STORIES THAT CREEP IN.

So like a game of chess, you find yourself constantly caught in a battle between 'GOOD' and 'BAD' thoughts and feelings.

I'M A NICE GUY.

I'M SELFISH.

You advance the 'Good Guys' across the board ...

I JUST GOT A
PROMOTION.

I HELPED MY
FRIENDS.

I'M GOING
TO THE GYM.

... only to find a whole army of 'Bad Guys' waiting to counterattack.

YOU BLEW THAT
PRESENTATION!

YOU MISSED YOUR
RUN ... YOU'RE LAZY!

YOUR FRIEND
HASN'T CALLED
YOU — HE
HATES YOU!

Trying to feel good about yourself through positive AFFIRMATIONS will have LIMITED success ...

I LOVE &
APPROVE
OF MYSELF!

I AM A
WONDERFUL
HUMAN BEING.

Firstly, you
are unlikely
to BELIEVE it
any more than
saying ...

I'M
SUPERMAN!

I'M
WONDER
WOMAN!

... secondly, even if what you're saying rings TRUE ...

I'M A KIND AND CARING PERSON.

I'M LOYAL AND TRUSTWORTHY.

your **THINKING SELF** will still come up with negative counter-argument: this always happens.

WHAT ABOUT *THAT* TIME?

YOU DON'T *ALWAYS* KEEP SECRETS.

EXERCISE

Repeat the following statements to yourself and notice what thoughts pop into your head in response:

I am a human being.

I am a worthwhile human being.

I am a lovable, worthwhile human being.

I am a competent, lovable worthwhile human being.

I am a perfect, competent, lovable, worthwhile human being.

YEAH, *RIGHT*!

WHO ARE YOU *KIDDING*?

STOP TALKING *RUBBISH*!

YOU *WISH*!

WHAT A JOKE!

Did you find the more POSITIVE the affirmation, the more NEGATIVELY your mind responded? Now let's REVERSE it and see what happens:

I AM A USELESS, WORTHLESS, UNVALUED PIECE OF HUMAN GARBAGE.

HANG ON A MINUTE: I'M NOT THAT BAD! NO WAY — I DON'T BELIEVE THAT!

The reality is we can waste a lot of time locked in this never-ending battle which is often FIERCE.

HOW COULD YOU BE SUCH AN IDIOT?

YOU'RE NOT AN IDIOT YOU JUST MADE A MISTAKE!

WHO ARE YOU KIDDING? LOOK AT LAST TIME.

BUT THIS TIME IS DIFFERENT! I'VE LEARNED MY LESSON.

YEAH RIGHT! YOU'LL ALWAYS STUFF IT UP!

NO I WON'T!

WILL TOO!

And while all your attention is on this BATTLE it's hard to connect with anything ELSE. You get lost in your thoughts instead of engaging in LIFE.

SO WHAT TO DO?

LEARN HOW TO BE LIKE THE CHESS BOARD. THE BOARD HOLDS THE PIECES BUT IT DOESN'T GET INVOLVED IN THE *BATTLE*!

HOW DO I DO THAT?

DEFUSION! UNHOOK YOURSELF FROM ALL THE STORIES — BOTH POSITIVE AND NEGATIVE. IF YOUR MIND TELLS YOU A NEGATIVE STORY, TRY THIS ...

I'M A LOSER.

THANKS MIND! THERE'S THE *'I'M NOT GOOD ENOUGH'* STORY.

And if your mind tells you a POSITIVE story ...

I'M WONDERFUL!

THANKS MIND! THERE'S THE *'I AM GOOD ENOUGH'* STORY!

Let your mind chatter away like a radio in the background ...

DOOM AND GLOOM

WONDER AND HOPE

... and engage fully in your LIFE.

GOOD ENOUGH

NOT GOOD ENOUGH

After all, at your funeral, would you want your loved ones to be thinking something like this ...

SHE WAS SO CARING AND LOVING AND KIND AND GENUINE.

... or this?

SHE HAD A REALLY HIGH OPINION OF HERSELF.

You are not who you think you are. So unhook from the story, and get PRESENT!

AND REMEMBER: THERE ARE TWO ESSENTIALS FOR MAKING LIFE RICH, FULL AND MEANINGFUL. ONE: *ENGAGE MINDFULLY* IN WHATEVER YOU ARE DOING. TWO: MAKE SURE WHAT YOU ARE DOING IS *MEANINGFUL*!

I KNOW HOW TO DO THE FIRST ONE, BUT HOW DO I DO THE SECOND?

YOU'LL FIND OUT IN THE NEXT PART OF THE BOOK.

Chapter 12

Follow your heart

In order to create a rich, full and meaningful life, it's important to reflect on WHAT WE'RE DOING and WHY WE'RE DOING IT.

It's time to ask some BIG QUESTIONS in order to clarify your VALUES.

▶ What is deeply important to you?

▶ What sort of person do you want to be?

▶ What sort of relationships do you want to build?

▶ If you weren't struggling with feelings and avoiding fears what would you channel your time and energy into doing?

VALUES are:

▶ our heart's deepest desires for how we want to behave, and what we stand for in life

▶ how we want to treat ourselves, others and the world around us.

When we live guided by values, we gain vitality and we experience life as RICH, FULL and MEANINGFUL — yes, even when it HURTS.

VALUES are not the same as GOALS.

VALUE	**GOAL**

I WANT TO BE *LOVING* AND *CARING*.

I WANT TO GET *MARRIED*.

VALUE

▶ How you want to behave, deep in your heart.

▶ A direction you want to keep moving in.

▶ An ongoing process with no end.

GOAL

▶ Something you want to get, complete, have, own, or achieve.

▶ Once achieved, it's over and done with; completed; 'ticked off the list'.

GOAL	**GOAL COMPLETED**	**WITH ONGOING VALUES**	**WITHOUT ONGOING VALUES**

I WANT A *BETTER* JOB.

YOU'RE *HIRED*.

I WANT TO BE *PRODUCTIVE*, *CREATIVE*, AND *RESPONSIBLE*.

I'LL SHOW UP TILL *HOME TIME*.

WHY ARE VALUES SO *IMPORTANT?*

LET ME INTRODUCE THE JEWISH PSYCHIATRIST *VIKTOR FRANKL.*

FRANKL SURVIVED AUSCHWITZ...

AND LATER WROTE...

MAN'S SEARCH FOR MEANING

...BASED ON HIS EXPERIENCES & OBSERVATIONS IN THE CAMP

IN PARTICULAR HE NOTICED THAT THOSE WHO SURVIVED THE LONGEST WERE OFTEN NOT THE *FITTEST* OR *STRONGEST*...

...BUT THOSE WHO HELD A SENSE OF *PURPOSE* &

MY CHILDREN!

FRANKL'S PURPOSE WAS HIS WIFE

I'LL SEE HER AGAIN!

I'LL KEEP GOING FOR HER!

AND HIS *VALUES* GAVE HIM *MEANING* EVEN THROUGH THE *HORRORS*

I'LL TELL THIS TO THE WORLD!

AND *SOMETHING TO LIVE FOR!*

HOLD ON JOSEF!

WHILE THOSE WITHOUT LOST THE WILL TO *LIVE!*

Life can be HARD WORK. Anything meaningful brings CHALLENGES. Often this leads us to give up or quit.

IT'S *TOO* HARD.

I'M NOT EVEN *GOING THERE!*

VALUES make the EFFORT worthwhile.

If your values are:

CONNECTING WITH NATURE	**BEING A LOVING PARENT**	**SELF-CARE**

... you'll make the trek.	... you'll make time to play with your kids.	... you'll exercise and eat well.

But what if (like so many, not just those who are depressed) you think:

WHAT'S THE *POINT*?

IS THAT *ALL* THERE IS?

I HAVE *NOTHING* TO OFFER.

SOMETIMES I DON'T WANT TO *LIVE* ANYMORE.

Even THEN, values can give your life PURPOSE and MEANING.

EXERCISE

Imagine that you're 80 years old.

Now finish the following sentences:

▶ I spent too much time worrying about ...

▶ I spent too little time doing things such as ...

▶ If I could go back in time I would ...

NOW NOTICE — ARE THOSE *DEMONS* COMING BACK ON THE DECK OF THE BOAT?

YES!

THOUGHT DEMONS

I'm a hypocrite!
I'll fail!
It's too late!
I can't change!
I'm too busy!
I'm too tired!
I shouldn't have to!

FEELING DEMONS

Anxiety
Confusion
Guilt
Frustration
Fear
Shame
Regret
Embarrassment

SO DROP ANCHOR!

HOW?

UNHOOK FROM THE THOUGHTS. *MAKE ROOM* FOR THE FEELINGS AND GET *PRESENT*! IN OTHER WORDS: *DEFUSE*, *EXPAND*, AND *CONNECT*.

What do you really WANT?

TO BE *HAPPY*

TO BE *RICH*

TO BE *SUCCESSFUL*

A GREAT *JOB*

SOMEONE TO *LOVE* ME

TO *MARRY* AND HAVE *KIDS*

These answers are not VALUES — they are all GOALS. To help you clarify VALUES, please do the exercise in the next chapter.

And remember: the PAST doesn't exist — it's just MEMORIES in the PRESENT ...

... and the FUTURE doesn't exist either — it's just THOUGHTS and IMAGES in the PRESENT.

SO WHAT DOES THAT LEAVE YOU WITH?

NOW!

SO REMEMBER ...

... LIFE *GIVES* *MOST* TO THOSE WHO MAKE THE *MOST* OF WHAT LIFE *GIVES*!

Chapter 13

The 1000-mile journey

We're going to start this chapter a little differently to all the others: no cartoons, just an exercise on clarifying your values. Please complete it before reading the rest of the book; it's very important for everything that follows later.

EXERCISE: CLARIFY YOUR VALUES

Below are 40 of the most common values. Please read through the list and write a letter next to each value, based on how important it is to you:

V = very important

Q = quite important

N = not important

1. Acceptance/self-acceptance: to be accepting of myself, others, life, etc.

2. Adventure: to be adventurous; to actively explore novel or stimulating experiences

3. Assertiveness: to respectfully stand up for my rights and request what I want

4. Authenticity: to be authentic, genuine, and real; to be true to myself

5. Caring/self-care: to be caring toward myself, others, the environment, etc.

6. Compassion/self-compassion: to act kindly toward myself and others in pain

7. Connection: to engage fully in whatever I'm doing and be fully present with others

8. Contribution and generosity: to contribute, give, help, assist or share ☐

9. Cooperation: to be cooperative and collaborative with others ☐

10. Courage: to be courageous or brave; to persist in the face of fear, threat or difficulty ☐

11. Creativity: to be creative or innovative ☐

12. Curiosity: to be curious, open-minded, and interested; to explore and discover ☐

13. Encouragement: to encourage and reward behavior that I value in myself or others ☐

14. Excitement: to seek, create and engage in activities that are exciting or stimulating ☐

15. Fairness and justice: to be fair and just to myself or others ☐

16. Fitness: to maintain or improve or look after my physical and mental health ☐

17. Flexibility: to adjust and adapt readily to changing circumstances ☐

18. Freedom and independence: to choose how I live and help others do likewise ☐

19. Friendliness: to be friendly, companionable or agreeable toward others ☐

20. Forgiveness/self-forgiveness: to be forgiving toward myself or others

21. Fun and humour: to be fun loving; to seek, create and engage in fun-filled activities

22. Gratitude: to be grateful for and appreciative of myself, others and life

23. Honesty: to be honest, truthful and sincere with myself and others

24. Industry: to be industrious, hardworking and dedicated

25. Intimacy: to open up, reveal and share myself, emotionally or physically

26. Kindness: to be kind, considerate, nurturing, or caring toward myself or others

27. Love: to act lovingly or affectionately toward myself or others

28. Mindfulness: to be open to, engaged in and curious about the present moment

29. Order: to be orderly and organised

30. Persistence and commitment: to continue resolutely, despite problems or difficulties.

31. Respect/self-respect: to treat myself and others with care and consideration

32. Responsibility: to be responsible and accountable for my actions ☐

33. Safety and protection: to secure, protect or ensure my own safety or that of others ☐

34. Sensuality and pleasure: to create or enjoy pleasurable and sensual experiences ☐

35. Sexuality: to explore or express my sexuality ☐

36. Skilfulness: to continually practise and improve my skills and apply myself fully ☐

37. Supportiveness: to be supportive, helpful and available to myself or others ☐

38. Trust: to be trustworthy; to be loyal, faithful, sincere and reliable ☐

39. Other: .... ☐
....
....

40. Other: .... ☐
....
....

Adapted from *The Confidence Gap: From Fear to Freedom*, by Russ Harris, published by Penguin Group (Australia), Camberwell, 2010.

SO I'VE IDENTIFIED MY *VALUES — NOW WHAT?*

NOW YOU NEED TO TAKE *ACTION!* A MEANINGFUL LIFE DOESN'T JUST *HAPPEN* — YOU NEED TO *MAKE* IT HAPPEN!

LET'S BEGIN BY DIVIDING YOUR LIFE INTO *FOUR DOMAINS:*

1. HEALTH

Includes physical health, psychological health, spiritual health.

2. LEISURE

Includes fun and games — relaxation, sports, hobbies, creativity.

3. WORK/EDUCATION

Includes unpaid work (e.g. volunteering) and apprenticeships and self-education (e.g. reading books).

4. RELATIONSHIPS

Includes friends, family, neighbours, co-workers, etc.

NOTE: Start with one domain at a time or you'll get overwhelmed and give up. Over time, you can work through all of them.

SO HOW DO I START?

 THERE ARE FIVE STEPS IN SETTING MEANINGFUL GOALS:

STEP 1: SUMMARISE YOUR VALUES

Write down four or five of the most important values in this domain ...

IN MY RELATIONSHIP WITH MY WIFE MY VALUES ARE *LOVE, CARING, HONESTY* AND *SUPPORT.*

HEALTH — MY VALUES ARE *SELF-ENCOURAGEMENT* AND *SELF-COMPASSION.*

STEP 2: SET AN IMMEDIATE GOAL

Boost your confidence by starting with a SMALL, EASY goal — one that can be accomplished TODAY!

BE SPECIFIC

I'LL *RING* MY WIFE AND TELL HER I LOVE HER.

I'LL *WALK* FOR 10 MINUTES AT LUNCHTIME.

I'LL COOK A *HEALTHY DINNER.*

Remember: the journey of 1000 miles begins with a single step!

STEP 3: SET SOME SHORT-TERM GOALS

What are some small things you can do over the coming days or weeks that are consistent with your values?

I LIKE *HELPING OTHERS* BUT THIS JOB DOESN'T ALLOW IT ...

... SO I'LL SEARCH THE *INTERNET* FOR A MORE MEANINGFUL JOB.

Remember: lots of small steps ADD UP.

STEP 4: SET SOME MEDIUM-TERM GOALS

Now stretch yourself a bit further.
Remember: be SPECIFIC.

I VALUE TAKING CARE OF MY BODY — I'LL JOIN A *GYM* BY THE END OF THE MONTH.

I'LL COOK *HEALTHY RECIPES* THREE NIGHTS A WEEK.

I'LL TAKE A 20 MINUTE *WALK* EVERY DAY.

STEP 5: SET SOME LONG-TERM GOALS

WHAT CHALLENGES WILL TAKE ME IN MY *VALUED DIRECTION*?

WHAT WOULD I LIKE TO DO IN THE NEXT 6 MONTHS, 1 YEAR, 5 YEARS, ETC?

ACTION PLANS

Now break down your goals into an action plan.

▶ What smaller steps are required to complete this?

▶ What resources do I need?

▶ When, specifically, will I carry out these actions?

If your goal is to go to the gym three times a week your ACTION PLAN might be to:

Join the gym   **Get your gear together**   **Plan the times you'll go**

The RESOURCES you might need may be:

Money for membership ...   **... gym gear**   **... and a bag to put this in.**

Being SPECIFIC may involve:

You can:

- **change your goal**

- **make an ACTION PLAN to obtain the resources.**

Sometimes a resource is a SKILL:

MY GOAL IS TO IMPROVE RELATIONSHIPS BUT I DON'T KNOW *HOW*!

You can:

- **plan how you will learn the skill**
- **research/read, etc**
- **take a course.**

EXERCISE

Write down:

- a domain of life to work on
- your values in that domain
- goals (immediate, short, medium, long-term)
- your action plan for the immediate and short-term goals.

The GOOD NEWS is ...

THE MOMENT YOU START STEERING TOWARDS THE SHORE YOU'RE NO LONGER DRIFTING ALL AT SEA AND YOU CAN MAKE THE MOST OF THE JOURNEY ALONG THE WAY KNOWING YOU'RE FINALLY HEADING IN THE *RIGHT DIRECTION*!

Chapter 14

Finding fulfilment

IN A *VALUES-FOCUSED* LIFE YOU'RE MORE LIKELY TO ACHIEVE YOUR GOALS.

WHY?

BECAUSE IF YOUR *GOALS* ARE IN LINE WITH YOUR *VALUES*, YOU'RE MORE *MOTIVATED* TO PURSUE THEM!

PLUS — *CONNECTING WITH* AND *ACTING ON* YOUR VALUES CAN GIVE YOU FULFILMENT RIGHT NOW.

IN WHAT WAY?

SAY YOU WANT TO BUY A HOUSE — THAT'S YOUR *GOAL* — BUT YOU CAN'T AFFORD IT YET. WHY WOULD YOU PURSUE THAT GOAL?

TO PROVIDE *SECURITY* AND *TAKE CARE OF* MY FAMILY.

SO TAKING CARE OF THE FAMILY IS THE *CORE VALUE* HERE, YES?

YES.

WELL YOU CAN TAKE CARE OF YOUR FAMILY *ANYWAY*!

I SEE! I CAN STILL LIVE TO MY *VALUES* WHETHER OR NOT I GET THE *HOUSE*!

IF YOU BELIEVE YOU CAN'T BE HAPPY TILL YOU'VE ACHIEVED YOUR GOAL, LIFE WILL BE *MISERABLE*!

BUT I REALLY *WANT* THE HOUSE!

YOU DON'T HAVE TO GIVE UP ON YOUR *GOAL*! START SAVING!

SO I DON'T HAVE TO WAIT TILL I GET THE HOUSE TO HAVE THE SATISFACTION OF CARING FOR MY FAMILY.

Let's look at some other examples:

I WANT TO BE A DOCTOR BUT IT'S TEN YEARS OF *HARD SLOG*!

What is the CORE VALUE of that GOAL?

I'LL BE ABLE TO *HELP PEOPLE*!

There are many ways you can do that RIGHT NOW!

A common GOAL is to find a PARTNER ...

SIGH, I'M *LONELY*!

... and to be MISERABLE if you HAVEN'T!

TO BE *LOVING, CARING, SENSUAL* AND *FUN*!

So what is the CORE VALUE here?

BUT THAT'S NOT THE *SAME*!

You can still act on those values with FAMILY, FRIENDS — and YOURSELF.

No it's not, but you have a CHOICE ...

▶ to find meaning, here and now, in living by your values
or

▶ to be miserable by focusing on a goal you haven't achieved yet.

WHAT IF I *ACHIEVE* MY GOAL?

THERE'LL ALWAYS BE *SOMETHING ELSE* YOU WANT!

If you're always FOCUSED on GOALS, you will NEVER be content. However, your VALUES are ALWAYS available.

Chapter 15

A life of plenty

A beneficial by-product of creating a meaningful life is that POSITIVE EXPERIENCES will happen.

ISN'T THAT A *GOOD* THING?

OF COURSE — AND IT MAKES SENSE TO APPRECIATE THESE THINGS TO THE FULLEST WHILE YOU'RE EXPERIENCING THEM ...

... BUT MAKING THEM THE MAIN *GOAL* IN LIFE IS NOT HELPFUL.

HOW COME?

Because you'll end up back in the HAPPINESS TRAP!

The more you focus on having only PLEASANT FEELINGS ...

... the more you'll STRUGGLE against the UNPLEASANT ones.

THEN WHAT SHOULD I *DO* ABOUT *PLEASANT* FEELINGS?

BRING *MINDFULNESS* TO THEM!

EVERY DAY IS FULL OF OPPORTUNITIES TO *APPRECIATE* YOUR LIFE, EVEN WHILE YOU'RE *IMPROVING* IT!

BUT WE USUALLY DON'T EVEN *NOTICE* THESE THINGS.

WITH *MINDFULNESS* YOU CAN WAKE UP & EXPERIENCE ALL AROUND YOU!

HOW DO I DO *THAT*?

HERE ARE SOME WAYS ...

When you EAT, slow down and SAVOUR it.

TASTE it. Feel the SENSATIONS in your mouth.

If it RAINS, pay ATTENTION to it.

Hear the PITCH and VOLUME. Watch the PATTERNS it makes. SMELL the air.

When it's SUNNY, APPRECIATE it.

FEEL its WARMTH on your skin. See how everything BRIGHTENS.

· ·

When you hug, kiss or shake hands with someone, ENGAGE in it.

Notice how it feels. Let WARMTH and OPENNESS flow through you.

When you feel good, SAVOUR it.

Notice how it feels in your BODY. Notice all the SENSATIONS, THOUGHTS and IMAGES. APPRECIATE it.

Look into the eyes of a person you care about as if for the FIRST TIME.

OBSERVE everything about them — GESTURES, MOVEMENT, FEATURES.

Observe an ANIMAL with childlike CURIOSITY.

Take a familiar object and STUDY it as if you'd never seen such a thing before.

Before you get out of bed take TEN DEEP BREATHS.

See its COLOURS, MOVEMENTS, CONTOURS.

Use all your SENSES, appreciate its FUNCTION.

Notice the MOVEMENT of your lungs and feel wonder at how they give you LIFE.

As you connect with your values and act in accordance with them you may notice changes in OTHERS, too.

The more you act like the person you WANT TO BE ...

... the more you'll notice POSITIVE RESPONSES toward you.

ENJOY these responses. Be MINDFUL. Notice what is happening and APPRECIATE it.

When you act with OPENNESS, KINDNESS and ACCEPTANCE you'll probably receive the same ...

... MOST of the time!

(If not, go elsewhere!)

Savour POSITIVE INTERACTIONS and notice the ABUNDANCE in your life.

Build the CONNECTIONS by:

| EXPRESSING what you appreciate about others, life and yourself; | SHARING your difficulties and rewards; | LETTING OTHERS KNOW what they mean to you. |

 I LIKE THE WAY YOU DO THAT.

  CAN I TELL YOU ABOUT...?

  YOU'RE SUCH A *GOOD* *FRIEND*!

When you achieve goals that are in line with your values, there's often a pleasant emotion. Notice how it feels and ENJOY it — even the simple things.

THERE! IT'S *TIDY*.

A NICE, *HEALTHY* DINNER!

JUST A NOTE TO SAY HI!

It's all too easy to miss these things when the THINKING SELF tries to distract you with STORIES.

NOT GOOD ENOUGH!

MINDFULNESS

▶ awakens you to good things you may have taken for granted

▶ cultivates an attitude of openness and curiosity

▶ helps you to notice more opportunities

▶ provides stimulation and interest

▶ improves relationships

▶ increases fulfilment

▶ enables effective action.

NATURALLY IT'S EASIER TO BE MINDFUL WHEN LIFE IS GOING *SMOOTHLY*.

IN THE *TOUGH* TIMES, YOUR THOUGHTS WILL KEEP TRYING TO PULL YOU *OFF COURSE*.

THE IMPORTANT THING IS TO REMEMBER TO *PRACTISE* IT!

AND KEEP *CATCHING MYSELF* WHEN I GO OFF TRACK!

Chapter 16

Willingness

Say you've decided to climb a mountain because of the SPECTACULAR VIEW at the top.

Halfway up it's STEEP, NARROW and ROCKY.

You're COLD, TIRED and WET ...

... and you know it will only get WORSE.

I DIDN'T THINK IT WOULD BE *THIS* HARD!

But you're WILLING to endure this discomfort not because you WANT it or ENJOY it but because it's on the way to where you WANT to GO.

I'LL HAVE THE *SATISFACTION* OF MAKING IT AND SEEING THOSE *GREAT VIEWS*!

And say you want to write a book — you'll encounter many OBSTACLES ...

FUSION WITH UNPLEASANT THOUGHTS AND FEELINGS

I'LL NEVER SUCCEED.

I'M NOT *GOOD* ENOUGH.

WHAT IF I *FAIL*?

I FEEL *SCARED*.

PROCRASTINATION AND PUTTING OFF   or   **AVOIDANCE AND DISTRACTION**

THERE'S NO HURRY.

DEADLINE 1 WEEK!

I CAN'T THINK ABOUT IT NOW.

I NEED A DRINK.

You might finally
TAKE ACTION

... and give it
MEANING ...

... and acknowledge
that no matter
the outcome the
effort will be
WORTHWHILE.

But now you're
down to the NITTY
GRITTY and it's
getting HARDER.

You may be
tempted to BAIL
OUT ...

... that's where
WILLINGNESS
comes in.

WILLINGNESS MEANS

▶ making room for unpleasant thoughts and feelings in order to do something meaningful

▶ getting out of your comfort zone to do something you value.

WILLINGNESS DOESN'T MEAN YOU **LIKE, WANT** OR **APPROVE** OF UNPLEASANT THOUGHTS AND FEELINGS. IT MEANS YOU *ALLOW* THEM, SO YOU CAN DO WHAT MATTERS.

Willingness is something we practise in small ways every day ...

WHAT *THOUGHTS, FEELINGS, SENSATIONS* AND *URGES* AM I WILLING TO HAVE IN ORDER TO DO WHAT I *VALUE*?

To enjoy a movie you're willing to PAY for the ticket.

To go on holiday you are willing to PACK.

TIRED!

To pass an exam you're willing to STUDY.

Willingness is the only way to deal with OBSTACLES. When an obstacle presents itself you can say:

and your life stays stuck or gets smaller ...

OR

in which case there's no guarantee that life will get easier ...

or that there won't be another tougher or bigger obstacle down the road!

But by saying YES your life will get BIGGER.

HOW WILL MY LIFE *EXPAND* IF I STILL KEEP MEETING OBSTACLES?

BY SAYING YES YOU GAIN EXPERIENCE AND INNER STRENGTH. YOU *GROW* AS A PERSON!

If FINDING A PARTNER is important to you, along the way you'll experience:

And you might have some real DISAPPOINTMENTS!

Either you're WILLING to go through this or you're NOT.

HE WAS WORTH IT.

● ●

You might want to change to a more MEANINGFUL JOB ...

I WANTED *STATUS* AND *MONEY*. NOW I WANT TO *HELP* PEOPLE.

which might mean:

- less pay
- years of extra study
- parental disapproval.

But if you're WILLING you might reach your goal.

EXERCISE

Make a list of what you are willing to experience in order to reach your goal.

Now ask yourself:

ARE THERE ANY OF THESE I CAN'T *HANDLE?*

NO!

(provided you practise EXPANSION DEFUSION and CONNECTION)

WHAT WOULD BE USEFUL *REMINDERS?*

WHAT'S THE *SMALLEST, EASIEST* STEP I CAN BEGIN WITH?

AND *WHEN* WILL I BEGIN?

NOW!

Chapter 17

A meaningful life

You can apply the *ACT* principles to ANY area of your life you'd like to improve:

HEALTH LEISURE   **WORK/**   **RELATIONSHIPS**
                      EDUCATION

Whatever you're
doing, ENGAGE
FULLY with it.

Whoever you're
with be FULLY
PRESENT for them.

When unhelpful
thoughts arise
DEFUSE them.

Whenever
unpleasant feelings
arise MAKE
ROOM for them.

And whatever
your values are
be FAITHFUL
to them.

THE *ACT* SERENITY CHALLENGE

*Develop the courage to solve those problems
that can be solved, the serenity to accept
those problems that can't be solved and the
wisdom to know the difference.*

Adapted from the 'Serenity Prayer'

If your problems CAN be solved ...	If they CAN'T be solved ...	And be sure to practise CONNECTION.
SHORT OF CASH	DISABILITY	FOCUS *HERE* AND *NOW*
... take EFFECTIVE ACTION in line with your values.	... use DEFUSION, EXPANSION and CONNECTION to help you ACCEPT this.	

....

You can either **ACCEPT** *or* **take EFFECTIVE ACTION** *or* **do both simultaneously**.

....

And as you take action, ENGAGE FULLY in what you're doing. Act on your VALUES and pay attention to the effect your actions are having.

Remember, too: the PAST doesn't exist; it's just MEMORIES in the PRESENT. And the FUTURE doesn't exist; it's just THOUGHTS in the PRESENT.

SO WHAT DOES THAT LEAVE YOU WITH?

NOW!

REMEMBER: LIFE *GIVES MOST* TO THOSE WHO MAKE THE *MOST* OF WHAT LIFE *GIVES*!